Dialogue

Madina Zadeh

Acknowledgement

Firstly, I would like to thank Fattaneh for *who she is*. *Fattaneh* means *lovely*, and you really embody that with your kindness, giving spirit and big heart.

Secondly, I would like to thank Fattaneh as *my mother*. Truly, as a mother you are one of the most tenacious people I have ever known. I appreciate your wisdom, for still trying to learn, and your commitment to doing better for yourself and for others.

Because of these admirable traits, no matter how long this book took, you still believed in me and supported me with whatever you had. Although, I am not as natural as you are at writing, I hope this makes you proud.

Thank you for being here for me, mama.

Lots of love, Madina.

Thank You

To everybody who proofread, it's on you.

Glossary/Islamic beliefs:

- Hadith: A report or an account.

- Surah: Chapter

- The Hour: The time of reckoning, or the end of time, or in reference to the day of judgement.

- 'Peace and blessings of Allah be upon him' [transliteration in Arabic: sal Allahu alayhi wa salaam] is a short prayer that some scholars believe is mandatory to utter after saying prophet Muhammad's name (peace and blessings of Allah be upon him). This opinion partly stems from surah 33, Al-Ahzab, *The Combined Forces*, where Allah says, "Indeed, Allah showers His blessings upon the Prophet, and His angels do pray for him. O believers! Invoke Allah's blessings upon him, and salute him with worthy greetings of peace." (verse 33:56). However, other scholars hold the opinion that this is mandated upon a person once in a lifetime, while saying it is highly recommended to do as per the former opinion. Though, it is an issue of dispute, I follow the former opinion in this book.

- 'Peace be upon him/her' [transliteration in Arabic: alayhi salaam (for men) and alayha salaam (for women)] is a short prayer that can be uttered after anyone's name.

Asterisk and Em Dash:

Every poem/prose ends either with an em dash (—), or an asterisk (*) or with both.

Kind words and forgiveness are better than charity followed by injury. And Allah is Self-Sufficient, Most Forbearing.

[Surah Al-Baqara, 2:263, Quran]

Do you not see how Allah compares a good word to a good tree? Its root is firm and its branches reach the sky,
always yielding its fruit in every season by the Will of its Lord. This is how Allah sets forth parables for the people, so perhaps they will be mindful.
And the parable of an evil word is that of an evil tree, uprooted from the earth, having no stability.
Allah makes the believers steadfast with the firm Word of faith in this worldly life and the hereafter. And Allah leaves the wrong-doers to stray. For Allah does what He wills.

[Surah Ibrahim, 14:24-27, Qur'an]

Do not make a decision placing
a rock on your heart.
Make a decision placing
your trust in The Almighty.

Contents

Reign

One day
I will learn the words to
how you make me feel.

And if you deny it, then at least I will know what to say to help
others tell their truth.

— The Power of Language

You captured a bird that
knew how to fly.

You caged a bird whose
home had been the expert lands and generous sky.

You imprisoned a bird that
was loyal.

A bird that always had a choice even under
your control.

And one day the bird left
without needing the key you
always kept close.

In this is a lesson about
where real power lies.

— Intentions

I was patient until
patience turned into
oppression.

* *I put my voice down and*
   picked up my heart.
   Finally, choosing peace over you against
   me.

— Breakdown From Hair to Feet

And here I still was for a long time, foolishly
trying to make something beautiful out of
what I finally realised were
your selfish desires and
my act of blindness.

* *So, I opened my eyes, and
everything was beautiful again.*

I will not take another step with
this broken heart anymore.

I am taking back my love.
I am praying my way out of this.
I will no longer smile with a sick body.

My happiness has nothing to do with you anymore.

— Feeling Whole Again

Understand this:

One man will take from you, but
another will give even
when you're not looking.

One will notice and use you.
Another will love and learn from you.

One will pass time with your love, and
another will make a living out of it.

— Companion

I did unhealthy things to my body when
you would mistreat me.

I would bite the words on my tongue, or
break walls and windows with them.
My voice left scratches on every door in
the neighbourhood.
I would disturb my heart for long and
cry my eyes swollen.
I would burden my brain to my knees in
wake and sleep.

* *My body has recovered*
  from lessons rare to
  learn.

— Extraordinary Things

You made me of the women whose love died.
Of the women who felt uncomfortable in their own skin.
The women who cried and complained.
Those who cut their hair.
Who broke.
Forgot themselves.

You made me of the women who have a past.

* *I regressed in pursuit of you.*

— Starting Anew

How little you appreciated,
how much you wanted.
How little you trusted,
how much you took.
How little you learnt,
how much you used.
How little you cared,
how much you expected.
How little you wanted to change,
how much you made me try.

* *We were never in this together.*

He does not feel about you the
way he makes you feel about yourself:
worthy,
loved,
beautiful,
unique.

It's to make you feel for
him.

* *Manipulation can feel real too.*

Sometimes, I convince myself that
you loved me.
Other times, I fight myself that
you didn't.

It was hard to figure this out while
you were here.
It's exhausting doing this now that
you are gone.

And the truth is that you are
gone.

— Processing

I'm learning
lessons I
want to smoke on.
But I'm not.

I want to wash away watered down
promises with toxic drinks.
But I'm not.

I want to sleep it off on pills.
But I don't want to go through the pain later.

I'm avoiding strangers I
can take advantage of too.

I want to know how it feels like to
be the one who got away.

I'm fighting demons that
want to turn me into
you.

* *I win every day. And each day, you*
   seem less real to me.

My love did not make you love me.
It made you selfish.

My words did not make you understand.
It made you immovable.

You blamed me for getting hurt when
you'd hurt me.

You hated on me when
I needed to heal.

I no longer felt the human in
us.

— Unloved

As I fought harder, I lost my grace.
As I lost my grace, you lost your place.

Losing myself more than I had
wasn't an option.

Losing you, was.

* *Not everyone will understand that you're hurt when*
  you 'lose it'.

  You can talk, shout, type, cry and move your hands as
  desperately as
  your mouth, but no
  sooner could you hope for their compassion before they
  break you again and
  call you 'crazy'.

  Not everyone deserves to see you this raw.

  See your grace as your crown.
  Would you not choose your crown over someone who tips
  it over, expecting you to correct it each time?

  Know who to keep your crown on for and
  who you can take it down for.

— My Grace, My Crown

How many times you hurt me, and
I made myself happy again.

What you did was easy, but
what I did was hard.

You did not make me stronger.
I did.

* *Freedom of response gives you freedom from
people.*

When I told you to leave, the
whole universe opened the door for you
to go.

— Signs

As they grew in hurting you, you grew in loving them.

You were never in love with the pain.
You were just
forgiving.

So, don't question your sanity and standards, because
this is what forgiveness does:
it brings you closer to people who may not deserve you, until
what hurts you teaches you, and
what teaches you changes you.

— Long Awaited Answers

I don't know what I caught when
I lost you.

But it hurt everywhere.

It took me being sick to
get over you.

I'd recover a little, and then not again for
a long time.
Sometimes, I relapsed completely.

But I got better.
And before I knew it, I moved on as well.

I thought I had given up, but
sometimes, transition does not come through until you do.

— From Within

The more I saw you look at others, the less special I felt when you would look at me.

I was not jealous; you were not loyal.

You ended us many times.

I just had to leave.

— Unfaithful

You asked for depth but only dipped your fingers and feet.
Or maybe, I didn't have the treasures you
wanted to dive for.

You asked for passion but killed it.
Or maybe, you weren't in love.

You went from pursuing me with everything you had to
becoming a stranger when you had me.
Or maybe, I wasn't who you wanted to fight for.

You painted many beautiful pictures of our future together, but
eventually lost vision of everything.
Or maybe, I didn't fit the picture.

You had a list of plans before we even met, but
pretended like you didn't know what to do with me.
Or maybe, I couldn't make you care enough.

You gave your word, but
simply forgot.
Or maybe, lost interest.

* *You're not who I thought you were.*
  Or maybe, I wasn't the one.

Don't grieve over what they said.
Don't grieve over what they did.

You are not responsible for other people's actions.
You cannot control who people want to be.

You are only responsible for yourself, and
you are above everything that happened.

Stop replaying failed scenarios that put you through everything,
again and again.

Waiting for validation and the conversation that they don't want
to have will wreck your nervous system.

You have the right to grieve, but your health has a right over you
too.

— You Owe Yourself

People need to learn to apologise without falling
sick.

People need to learn to apologise without causing
trauma.

People need to learn to apologise with unconditional
validation.

People need to learn to apologise without taking
offence.

People need to learn to apologise without
manipulating.

People need to learn to apologise to
others.

— Conscience

Some love and hurt you at the same time.
Some wound and heal you at the same time.
Some leave and wait for you at the same time.

Some are who they don't want to be.

Whether you stay or leave, you
cannot make it better or worse.

This is a battle against themselves.
Not with you.

Don't add to a fight they need to win
alone.

You don't deserve to be amidst all this.
This is not for you to solve or to save.

— The Journey of Others

The problem is that the shallowest of men choose the
dreamiest of women with no solid intention.
This approach by the man hurts the
vision of the woman, because now she
will try for happiness
with a hollow of a man.

— A Filler

When you were obsessed, nothing could stop you from winning me over.

When you wanted to leave, you couldn't leave any sooner.

When I was breaking, it didn't bring you back.

You did as you pleased.

— I Fought and Followed

My heart broke loving you.
My back broke trying for you.
My mind broke trying to understand your right, your wrong and your love for me.

I stand, broken together.

* *If you can become this for someone else, you can become better for yourself.*

Some people take away your right to react.

They'll point the finger before you can.

They'll leave before you can.

Your sanity will feel invalidated by the second.
The betrayal will consume you.
Abandonment will keep you awake.
Reaching out will increase your agony, as you're gaslit or cut off.

Loved ones will eventually be there for you in silence, with
nothing more to say or to offer.

And you'll become calm in
your suffering.
You'll become beautiful in your patience.
Your slate will become clean.
And you will live again.

What awaits them, no one knows.

But what they choose is only a fleeting happiness.
The comfort of denial doesn't last for long.

* *Self-accountability secures
   what self-interest can't.*

— A Lifetime of Wins and Losses

I was packing my clothes, and I felt you stand close behind me—so close that I might have bumped into you, but I knew not to.

I continued to pack my clothes, and you went to the other room to hide your desperation.

I continued packing my clothes, and you walked back in and sat in our favourite spot to get my attention.

I told you how much you hurt me, and
I saw you dig your nail into your skin to
stay strong.

You tried to manipulate me at every point but refused to apologise.

You did not want to break, and
so, you pressed on with pride.

* *I packed my clothes and left.*

I told you that
time will pass and
I will overthink.

I told you that
days will pass and
I will break.

I told you that
nights will pass and
I will cry myself to sleep.

But your silence was deafening.
You gave me distance when I needed you close.

Who knew that
scars would become a map to
find myself?

Who knew that
breaking has another end
that is strength?

— The Far Bright Side

Sometimes, you have to learn how to be human again.

To feel the pain that no one allowed you to feel.
To cry the tears that you were made to feel ashamed of.
To realise everything that was denied.

To live and not be stunted.
To be free and not be forced.
To be happy, however you choose.
To not be mocked for your ways.
To not be shut down.

To love and be loved without excuses, while making forgiveness a priority.

To breathe again.

— After Everything

In return for all the hurt, you
want to give them ownership over
your healing.

They don't deserve something so fortunate in exchange for
all the misfortunes they put you through.

You should own the struggles of your healing.
Don't hand it over to someone who only wants to take credit for
it.

* *This is your soft and messy journey.*

He was skilled at making me uncomfortable in
a second.

The words coming out of his mouth
tied my insides in a knot.

My tongue was pinned down by an invisible force.

It was hard to think after he spoke.

The shaming was paralysing.

It was a fight against a power I could not see.

Word by word, I
broke down.

* *You don't know what people are capable of projecting.
So, you need to be sure of yourself.*

It was like I was trying to speak a language that
I could never learn.

I ran in and out of
one maze after another.

Like my heart was
in a close race between
life and death.

I turned many unknown corners and
sweat countless chances.

How grateful I am to just be tired and dazed but
still safe and sane
after all this, and
you.

— Resilience

After you broke my heart, you moved
to my head and
broke me there too.

* *I know how to heal from*
  the most breakable of
  places.

We meet people with excuses instead of
with love for us.

So, we learn to make excuses for them too, forgetting
what we once wanted.

And sometimes, we remember again, because
amidst all the hurt we begin to feel lost.

— Our Years

All those words you did not reply to have finally
received their response in
your silence.

Everything you didn't love no
longer need your validation.

Everything that was never enough for you feel
at their best now.

This heart you broke has
finally broken away from you.

— At Peace

I have loved a dark heart before, and
it wants the same love as
a good heart but
with no questions asked.

— Love, Selfish

If I see you happy after
you leave, it
won't bother me.
It will encourage me to
be happier and
even grateful, knowing that
I'm not losing out.

If I see you at peace after
everything I went through, I
won't worry.
It will encourage me to
be at peace too, and
most importantly to move on.

I will choose me like
you choose yourself.

* *I will not live with your ghost.*

We think that we will be loved better because
of our past.

We think that we will gain someone's empathy, be understood,
and that this will finally set us free from
all the pain.

And so, we rely on different, but the same people all over again.
We get hurt all over again.

All at the cost of wanting to be loved at a time when we are most
vulnerable.

* *Personal space can be larger than life.*

Not every apology is an apology.

Sometimes, it's to mask something.

It can be to shut you up, so
they can carry on another time.

Sorry can be used to keep you.

Sorry may not take your forgiveness seriously.

Sometimes, an apology is anything but.

— Sorry

Don't hate on someone you
hurt.

They can't mend the pain at
your command.

They can't stop the tears that are
making you feel sick.

They can't move on because
you're ready to.

Don't hate on someone you
hurt.

*If you want to move on together, validate.

Today, you are trying your best to
convince me that
it all means nothing to you.

Tomorrow, you will spend a lifetime telling
your own daughter that
if a man truly loves you, he
will not look anywhere else.

* *When it's your turn to take care of
a girl like me.*

This guy?! This guy loves you! But in all the wrong ways. This guy thinks about you, but with no greater purpose. This guy. This guy talks but does nothing about it, because he doesn't mean it. This guy knows, but his arrogance knows him better. This guy. This guy will do it all, but only to win. What happens to you afterwards is irrelevant. You are this guy's dream, but he is incomplete. You have made this guy feel, but he is embarrassed by it—his ego is hurt. This guy is learning from you but will not acknowledge it—he is full of himself. He is still surprised about you, but is ignoring it, because it's easier this way. This guy knows how you feel about him, but is spoiling himself with it from afar. This guy is waiting for you to let him come close, so he can get what he wants even if you have to carry the pain forever. This guy is looking for something real, but easy. This guy. This guy will be sorry, because this is how he gets away with everything. This guy wants you with no strings attached.

* *He will fill your youth with scars.*

If I only give, will
you only take?

If I'm quiet about it, will
you ignore it too?

If I don't mention it, will
you not be grateful?

If I let it go, will
you not be sorry?

If I stop thinking about myself, will
you too?

If night comes, will
you let me sleep like this?

Life may be difficult, but
will you be too?

— Accountability

It hurt that
you believed in the possibility of
moving on while you had me, and that
you did not believe in love in
all its conditions.

But it hurt most that you were open about this, and I listened
and still chose you in the hope that you'd change your mind.

* *Don't bring it on yourself.*

I express and explain the hurt in me to
you.
I give you reasons for why you make me feel these unpleasant
ways, but
you behave like you are unsure, or even unaware of what I am
saying.

And while pretending this confusion, you silence me, turn me
down, and
get away with what you do.

— Denial

How to put a woman to sleep:

Say what she wants to hear.
Be sweet.
Love her.
Open her up.
Get her excited for the rest.

Change.
Deprive her.
Become someone else.
Because now, she will work hard for those things.

* *Nightmares don't come true.*
  It all happens in real life, so
  we can do something about it.

The truth is effortless.
You don't need to try and
remember.

Telling a lie is hard work.
Once through the teeth, it's under heavy control, or
ruined by a slip.

The lies I found out.

You were a loss that my heart could not let go of suddenly.

I had to realise to let go of you.
I had to learn to let go of you.

And that's... how I let go of you.

As simple and as difficult as that.
As invisible and visible as that.

— Loss

Trust issues:

They have not been taught to *trust*, and
they are not going to learn from your *loyalty,* no
matter how beautiful it may be.

They were taught to *question*, *control* and *possess*.

You both have different ways of
feeling secure within oneself and
in each other.

One gives peace, and
the other destroys for
their own peace.

— Trust

I did not speak out of nothing.
My sanity is a witness to this.

I did not cry for no reason.
You are a witness to this.

I did not fight to be difficult.
Everybody is witness to this.

You were behind everything I did, pretending
you had nothing to do with it.

— Gaslighting

You took me all the way and
gave me up in the end, which
none of us saw coming.

I had to walk it back alone, and it
felt longer and more painful than
when we walked it together through everything.

* *Time can become a never-ending emotion long after
  something is over.*

Thank you for putting yourself aside and
letting me go, because
you want me to be happy, but most importantly, so you can
have some peace too.

Thank you for putting yourself aside instead of
continuing to hurt me, because
you've finally had enough.

Thank you for making the right decision because
you no longer want to be sorry.

And I'm sorry that I'm upset, because
I fought for myself a long time ago, but
you made me believe in us.

Thank you for doing right by me now that
you are ready, and
I am at loss.

— If It wasn't for You

This love broke us.

Words went unheard.
Tears ended up on pillows.
Trying stopped midway.
Everything we had ended up in the past.

* *Nothing is left but healing.*

Sometimes, what has gone by only
runs further and faster away.

It's important to focus on what we still have to
make the changes we want.

* *What we have can be as valuable as what we lost.*

As cold as
you treated me and
as warm as
I treated you created
this hurricane after
my name.

— Her Mark

You took this last chance and
showed me how the rest of my life would be like.

I told you this was your *last chance*.

You set the tone for disappointment.

You didn't think I would do anything about it this time.

* *I went back to spend more time with myself, buy that*
  meal deal and the deck of play cards you
  made me put back.

One of the most heart-breaking experiences was
when I watched someone who hurt me move on like
we both got hurt.

This is entitlement.

I could only live through it, until
I wanted to live for myself again.

— Also Entitled

You were mistaken with the freedom I gave you.
You were supposed to love me like
I loved you.

But your heart wasn't built like
mine.
It catered to your fickle mind.

You lost yourself in
my trust, losing sight of
what's worth it and
what's not.

You entertained others at the decline of us, becoming more
absent to be everywhere else.
Forgetting the one who gave you the privilege to
behave like this.

— Boundaries

I can see the guilt on your face, but
not in your actions.

You think this makes you tough, but
it shows your insecurity.

While you're puffing up, you're shrinking in my eyes.

Real strength is in owning up, not pretending like you still own it
all.

* *Accountability is the new muscle.*

You controlled your love to
control me.

You rewarded me with affection instead of
giving it unconditionally.

You did not trust me, so
that you could trust us.

* *You thought this would keep me.*

You have to take a step back.

You have to take your dreams back.

You have to take your story back.

You have to be confident when
you leave toxic people behind.

— Growth

I've been destroying a place inside of me for
a long time now.
I realise that I am only helping you live there longer.

* *What needs acceptance should not be repressed.*
  What needs time should not be rushed.
  What needs consoling should not be punished.

  Your body will eventually get rid of what doesn't belong
  to you anymore.

You can't fix someone who
is broken.
You can only be there for them.

You can't fix someone who
doesn't want to be fixed.
You can only remind them of
what's better.

You can definitely not fix someone who
wants to break you too.
You can only leave.

* *Not everybody recognises that they need help.*

We sign up for people not knowing they're
projects.

Kindness triggers them.
They fight your love.
Good things are turned into tragedies.

We shouldn't judge their needs, but
at one point, you have tried enough to know that
you are enabling them.

They need to do better for themselves, and
you need to choose better for yourself.

* *You're not the problem, but you can be the solution.*

When anger talks, no one else speaks.
When pride wins, love loses.
When greed takes over, people lose each other.

Petals and thorns can make flowers, but
love and vanity can never make something
as beautiful.

— Many Lose Like This

Without responsibility love won't go far.
You can't sit and love someone.
You can't be absent and love someone.
You can't forget and love someone.

— Neglect

You ask how I am long after
our last conversation.
"Alive.", I answer.
And you seem satisfied, not
wanting to know more.

* *Closure is often as overrated as the person who
  left. You're not missing out on anything.*

— Move On

I asked for nothing and
that's what you gave me.

So, I gave you more of
what you didn't appreciate.

I stayed within the distance you
kept me at.

* *I didn't know that would be
the last time I'd tell you that I'm leaving, because
you let me.*

— Reciprocation

You could no longer waste my time when
I asked you for what I deserved.

So, you left, claiming
that I deserve better, blaming
yourself for this.

It hurts knowing that
you would have stayed longer if
I gave you access without
committing to me.

* *It was convenient until I
asked for something real.*

It's okay to be sensitive, but not over someone's preferences.
Don't put yourself ahead of others every time they
talk, feel, or want something different.

Sometimes, be strong
for others.

* *Let others be sensitive too.*

I trusted you more than I loved you.

I made myself vulnerable before you made me feel
safe.

Vulnerability reciprocates vulnerability, but
you gathered information on me.

You opened me up to pull the strings when you needed to.

I knew you like everyone else, but you were not who everyone
thought you were.

I got scared.
Our lives together were secrets I
didn't know about.

You kept me in the dark and
things took an ugly turn when
I found out.

* I will not wait for you to own up.

You taught me how to
put up a front on
my flaws.
You made me best at
keeping silent.
You taught me to
live life unresolved.

I learnt to think wrong.

I learnt not to stop even if
I'm at fault.
I learnt how to fight someone who
is right.

I learnt to listen like the dead.

I learnt to say things that I do not mean—good or bad.

I learnt to be difficult.

I learnt how to find someone real to
get my way, then leave them behind.

I learnt how to put everything important last, because
I learnt to lie to myself.

I learnt to care less.

You changed what was in my nature, but
nature always finds a way back.

* *I am unlearning you.*

Those who neither love you nor leave you will teach you how to do both.

— Gains

Never mind that you did not give us a chance at our lives together before you changed.

Never mind that I still stayed.

Never mind that I tried to reach out to you many times.

Never mind that you only grew more distant.

Never mind that you couldn't be alone with me.

Never mind that you weren't happy with anything I did.

Never mind that I didn't feel seen.

Never mind that you couldn't comfort me because it was against your nature.

Never mind that you wouldn't try unless I made you.

Never mind that you'd only love me when I wasn't myself.

Never mind that I communicated.

Never mind that you were always the victim.

Never mind that I tried to change myself.

Never mind that you always convinced me that nothing was wrong except for my reactions.

Never mind because you finally realised everything, but pointed your finger at me, as you couldn't defend yourself anymore and blamed it on the very problems I was trying to solve.

Never mind that your final move was to throw me on the line. Never mind that you left me totally defenceless, taking away from everything I did for us.

Never mind that I'm suffering for my part and for yours, because you can't face them, and I have no choice but to face it all.

Never mind, because I'm no longer dealing with everything that went wrong but with the pain of my sanity.

* *Never mind that I didn't see this coming.*

And after everything that they know you are, they still left.

You deserve better.
Behave like it.
Breathe like it.
Better is coming.

— To Better Days

Do you know what it feels like to be a natural at something?

That's how I feel at
being human.

— Women

When I told you that I will love you with all your flaws, it did not mean that
you could wrong me.

* *To be flawed is to be human, but to be human is to learn from your flaws.*

Understand that acknowledgement does not always come from
the person you shared the truth with.

You know the truth, and
sometimes, this has to be enough to
give you the peace you are seeking from
a liar.

They do not need to be on your journey of
validating what happened to you.
You can set yourself free from
everything they denied.

The truth exists with or
without them.

And one day, you need to care less for
their word and
appreciate this independence.

* *This is the truth.*

We were supposed to be best friends, until
one of us wanted it all and the other did it all.

It was us against the problem, until
one of us made the move against
the other.

We were together, until
one of us broke the other.

* *I didn't know things were so bad.*

I put up with strange things.

You'd call me crazy for reacting
to disrespect.

You'd accuse me of
being temperamental when
I'd call out your disrespect.

You'd pick a fight when
I would communicate.

You'd end a conversation when
it would be my turn to speak.

You'd give me distance and
call it 'space' when I was hurting.

You'd tell me that
we should both try to
make things work, as if
I was part of the problem.

* *I was not accountable for your mistakes.*

You felt like a jagged rock
lodged in my throat when
we parted ways.

Grieving you was difficult.

* *But it was worse being with you.*

Your tears come down faster than when you hurt me.
You silence me before I can tell you what's wrong.

I hear your voice inside my head, telling
me to be okay, non-stop.

I have no choice but to watch you pretend that
nothing has happened while you beg me to believe it, too.

I want to cry too, but
you force yourself to cry more.
I am trying to speak too, but
you talk faster and louder.
I am trying to feel too, but
we've already broken down.

It's another horror scene for being the one who is hurt.

— I Can't Hear Myself

I'm sorry that I could not pick you up when
you fell to your knees, for
what I did was more fallen than
I had the courage to admit.

I'm sorry that I shouted over your wails because I didn't want
you to feel so betrayed.

I'm sorry that I took your cover off to
cover for myself, but it came natural to me.

I'm sorry that I could not hold you when you became too weak
to cry, because I was fighting for my dignity.

I'm sorry that I still showed up and
took from you, knowing that I would not stay.

I'm sorry that I continued to hurt you, but it was over for me, so
it didn't mean to me what it still meant to you.

I'm sorry that I knew you weren't doing so well, but
that's all I felt like any average stranger.

I'm sorry that you were still there while
I moved on.

I'm sorry that you lost so badly.

I'm sorry that I couldn't have the conversation that hurt me too
much to have.

I'm sorry that you questioned if anything was ever real between
us.

I'm sorry, but I was afraid of us and of
you.

I'm sorry, but I was afraid of disappointing again.

I'm sorry that only in the end
did I wish I could take all your pain away.

I'm sorry that you had to go through this the hard way.

* *The hard way is not doomed, it leads
to another way.*

I thought I'd be happy if
one day I found out that
you're going through what
I went through.
But the thought of you or anyone enduring such pain scared me.

So, I questioned myself that if justice would be served by you
going to hell, would I want that? And I didn't.

So, I thought of something that felt closer to home: one's organs
being removed and traded by the hands of someone you trust.
It sent chills down my spine even
for my enemies.

So, I don't know how you never hesitated to hurt me in all the
ways you did.

One day, it all came back to me, and I could barely sit up.
I desperately prayed for the pain to be replaced with happiness.
And you were still on my mind.
I hesitantly said your name too.
And before I could finish my prayer, it was as if someone blew
life into my heart.

I could not deny the sudden joy and peace I felt.
My heart became like a weightless balloon.

I waited for the feelings to leave, but
they didn't.

Allah had made it this easy all along.
I needed the miracle to forgive you to
receive all other miracles.

* *It's okay to forgive the cruel things in life for your own peace.*

I wailed my heart out of my mouth.

If anyone knew how hurt I was, it was me.
If anyone knew how to hurt me, it was you.

What I didn't know was that
you were never going to stop.

What you didn't know was that
I could make it stop.

* *The moment I knew better.*

Please.
I am not made for
lonely people.
Do not use me to fill a hole in your life so
deep that I lose myself.

Please.
I am not made to
make your past better.
Do not use me as mere distraction, worthy of
nothing more.

Please.
I am not made for someone's whim devoid of accountability.

* *Do not compress me on your wounds.*

No one is going to talk to you like
I did.
I spoke to you whether
you loved or hurt me.

* *Communication was not your*
 love language. Silence was not mine.

— Censorship

I hope that years down the line the
details of our love remain
the same.

That we'll find out about each other as
we grow.
That we'll endure.
That we would do it all over again.

* *What is real needs to be taken care of too.*

The heartbreak set my head on fire, like a burning cold.

It inflamed my airways, like a burning cold.

It made my joints ache, like a burning cold.

It attacked my chest, like a burning cold.

It made me weak, like a burning cold.

It made my eyes runny, like a burning cold.

And there is no cure for a burning cold other than
rest and time.

So, I burnt, resting.

I passed time, burning.

— Spring

A person who is there but
not there for you
will make you lonely.

They'll give you hope and
crush it in the same breath.

Waiting will become a way of life.

The time you lose
will not bring them back
to you.

— Forgotten Loved Ones

You remained the same after
every apology and
changed me all along.

— Growing Apart

Tell me,
what do you want from me
after all that happened?

How can I hurt you when
you are already hurt?
What am I going to do with a revenge like this?

I can only hope better for you, so that maybe when
you reach your peak and feel the emptiness of it, you
understand what always mattered and what
doesn't.

* *When the world will not be enough.*

Your love felt so real that
I became vulnerable.

I felt purified. Reborn. Soft.
I was learning to live.

But you took everything back and made me watch while doing
so.

I stood stripped because
I trusted you.

I became the talk of every circle.

The closest people conveniently began living their
own lives.

Some said I was possessed and
it took over you.

I came to you about everything, but you were neither on their
side, nor
on mine.

You wanted nothing to do with me.

I will never forget our young, striking faces.
Your puppy eyes and my dreamy gaze.
How fiercely you chose me and how spoilt I was.
The way you looked in every suit and how I dressed up for you.

I will never forget how right you made us feel, even during the
worst times.

Little did I know that
you were trying so hard because you had so much to hide.

* *I remember like it was*
yesterday when everything
changed. But with time I've learnt to live with it better.
The pain that used to drown me now dissolves, and no one can
tell that something so dark and deadly turned into
understanding, empathy, humility, growth, forgiveness, wisdom,
light, and a new life.

I still want to open your chest and see if you really meant to hurt me like this.

Did you mean to target everything that would never let me go back to normal life?

Did you mean to hate on me so hard that I'm left with nothing to warm myself with?

Did you mean to suffocate me wherever I go, in whatever I do?

Did you mean to wage a war against my sanity?

Did you mean to shake me with terror?

Did you mean to leave me?

I'd like to believe that you didn't mean any of it, and that I suffered for no reason, so we can be together again.

* *We don't need much to feel loved.*
  But sometimes, no amount of
  inflicted pain can make us understand that we are not loved
  somewhere.

They are not afraid of losing you.
They are afraid of losing you to others.

Love can become jealous.
But jealousy can never love.

— Entitlement

My heart and body became one in
feeling the aches.

The world around me glitched as
I became desperate for help.

Every face I turned to had changed.

I was still me, but in a different reality.

The notion of time seemed to have perished, feeling like forever.

But the transformation from such suffering was
also inevitable.

— A Heart Settled In Faith

You managed quite well, but
I suffered just to manage with the basics.

I don't know how much you've lived since we parted ways, but
what's supposed to be easy was difficult doing them with fresh
wounds.

Your hands alone are strong enough, but my entire build was
too soft to withstand it all.

I experienced something beyond breaking, which set me free.

They say that love can make you feel like you're in heaven.
So, sometimes, it's suffering that makes you want the real place.

The little box of pain you gave me came with ever-lasting gifts I
could only dream of.

* *I always wanted to live a little big.*

They hurt you, but
you still thanked them for
everything in the end.

— The Miracles of Life.

I remember us, and
I feel betrayed.

I remember meeting our family and friends, and
I feel betrayed.

I remember the places I showed you, and
I feel betrayed.

I remember everything we laughed and cried over, and
I feel betrayed.

I remember everything we
fought for, and
I feel betrayed.

I remember you having me vulnerable, and
I feel betrayed.

I remember when everything got too real for you, and
I feel betrayed.

I don't know when you realised that you were in two hearts
about us.

I don't know if you were lying to yourself about me all along.

I became sick with
trying to figure out what was real and what wasn't after
you left.

It was a vicious cycle.

I had to stop the conversations with people.
I had to stop the thoughts when alone.

The versions of what I believe in still change every now and then.

Whatever the truth is, I tried to find out from you, but nothing made sense.

I don't know if you really wanted to leave, or if maybe, in the end, you realised you didn't want to, but still did.

I don't know.

Sometimes, I feel like a lost child looking for answers.
Were you helpless?
Did you have reasons I would not understand?
Or were you just selfish and didn't know how to tell me without losing face?

I don't know.
But I'm trying to make the best out of everything.

I'm carrying on as you decided to.

And while doing so, I'm only hoping from my Lord because in the end, our return is to Him, no matter what we lose or gain here.

** Everything will perish except for
Allah.*

You made my heart heavy instead of
full.

I carried it and
couldn't let go.

It became toxic inside of me and
between us.

I don't blame you for having made me believe that you could
have made me happy.
I blame you for not listening whenever I
needed you to.

— Something You Don't Want to Hear

The pain you gave me
I could use against your life, but
I chose to forgive you.

— Freedom

People stick around long and hard because of love, but also for benefits.

Know people as
they know you.

Don't ignore the obvious.

* *Sometimes, it's important to
know better than to love harder.*

I spent too much time with my feelings over you long after you left.

While you were building, learning, and getting smarter, I stayed stuck in the past for far too long, ruminating over everything that happened, and coming up with new questions and conversations, alone.

How did I lose so much pride in myself?

I thank Allah for hearing my cries that
you walked away from.

* *It won't get better one day. It gets better on random days and in random moments. You will get through this with Allah by your side the whole time, not just for one day.*

Now that you are secure, you are ready for
me.

But I was ready for you when we had nothing.

I was ready for you when everything went down between us.

I was ready for you when you left.

I was ready for you when you knew I was not okay.

I was ready for you when history repeated itself.

Now that you are ready, I'm not.

I don't want what you've earned.

It would have been more honourable had you made things right
with nothing to your name but the promises you made me.

It would have been more real had you apologised when you
were vulnerable.

It would have been more humane had you not left to build your
life while I dug myself out of the rubble.

* *You are too late, because healing hurts more.*

You didn't sound right.
You spoke like a stranger and
seemed so unfamiliar.

It felt unsettling
because my gut wanted to know you
as you should know someone you've been close with for
so long.
But I was forcing it.

And what do you say to a stranger anymore?
I love you?
Do you remember when?
You disappointed me?
Give details?
Or just cry?
A stranger would think you're crazy and run away.

You ran away
and I thought I was crazy for believing that I knew you and
for trying so hard to tell you about everything we had, and what
went wrong.

* *You never showed your face again, and that's a confession.*

You polluted the bottom of
my heart.

But like water, emotions run deep and to faraway places.
So, this poison will make its way back to you because you will
not be able to live without what your own hands have
corrupted.

* *I will clean my origin and return purer.*

— The Circle of Life

Save a Marriage, Not a Monster

She gave you chances, child, after
child, after child.
Such noble chances. Such precious chances. Such sincere
chances.

So much was put into a better fate:
Prayer. Heart. Body. Soul.

But...
you chose to be stubborn with those who
were most vulnerable.
You did not recognise what you had. You only ever recognised
yourself: an immovable pride.
You did not care. You only covered for yourself: a flaw of your
culture.
You did not want to know better: a disease of your mind.

* *Dear woman,*
  a child is not a means to
  change a toxic partner or to
  fix a relationship.

  If he does not deserve you,
  how can he deserve
  more than you?

  Having a child to make
  someone worthy is
  not praiseworthy.

  Putting a child on the line
  does not make you
  courageous.

*Playing with innocence does
not make you great.*

*You will end up giving away
the milk in your bones
because bleeding will not be
enough.*

*Begging and breaking
yourself do not make you a
dream woman.*

*Stop worshipping
relationships.
It's not romantic.*

Someone who does not have a mind of their own will break yours.

They will take what you both have and
throw it in the mouths of
those who
talk.

They'll give your rights away to family and strangers; always serving others with more of you—changing according to the crowd.

A person who does not have a mind of their own will break yours, not knowing what to do with you. And letting others.

* *Sometimes, you lose yourself in less obvious ways.*

You demanded that I behave, and
it was so difficult.

To be good when
you were loose.

To love when
you weren't there.

To believe, knowing
about the lies.

To not cry, nor fight back, or walk away
when you were hurting me.

To keep quiet and
stay.

To try, knowing
that you don't care.

To leave when
I didn't want to but
had to.

* *You did not even deserve to know my
  name.*

You expect her to notice when
you're trying, but not when
you're a monster.

You expect her to hear you out, but
not when she needs the same.

You expect her to understand when
you make mistakes, but not that
she's also imperfect.

You expect her to accept that
you're sorry, but not that
you're lying.

* *Expect nothing but to lose her.*

You made me tired of hurting and crying.

I made you tired of calling and trying, so
it would no longer be worth taking from me anymore.

We were always talking at the doorstep.
I'd always go back in without you.

I could no longer live in suspense being
married to you.

— Go No Contact

I've had enough of
feeling insecure.

You laughed your days away at me whenever
you felt like a loser.

You put down everything that
you loved, admired, but envied.

Another day, another round against
me.

I tried smiling it off, but it
still put you in a bad mood.

I tried keeping quiet, so
it could pass by faster than
when I'd fight.

I tried to love more
than anything.

I tried to keep us, but
I fell apart
only to get back with you.

You carried on, got carried away, and
I carried myself.

— With Confidence

They did not hold on to you. They had a hold on you.

They did not want you. They felt entitled to you.

They always left the
door behind them open to
come back for more.

— Abusive Presence

Prison techniques were used on me.

My spirit was broken, so
I could no longer believe in myself.

I was made afraid to think.

I reached a point where I doubted
right from wrong.

I became absent in my body, disabled
from anything done to me, and
unmoved by anything said.

I was made to forget my worth, so
I could never find my way back.

It took a lot of courage to
come out human again.

— For The Human in Me

Someone who truly deserves you will never
give up on you.
Someone who loves you will always
be there.
Someone who wants you will never
leave.

Someone who is stubborn will never
give up on you either.
Someone who controls will always
be there too.
Someone who abuses will also never
leave.

* *History means little without character.*

I have been broken to boredom.
I blank out at your blows. The look in my eyes scare you
because it looks like nothing anymore.
My silence triggers you more than
when I used to shout.
You're trying to wind me up, but you give up, get tired, almost
cursing yourself.
I'm not 'crazy' now, but I still drive you out of your mind.

You're finding it easier to love me to
test if I will be me again, so you can be you, and
I get back to emotional labour.

While you're doing everything to
make me stay and get away, I
am the one who no longer wants you.
You don't scare me anymore.
I save and endanger people like you.

* *I'll be gone while you think that
   you're planning my lonely end.*

Words,
silence,
words,
silence,
words,
silence,
words,
silence
ticked the *second hand*.

The clock was not broken. I was;
talking to someone who
was never there.

Time is precious, and as your *second hand*
this made me painfully aware of
every passing moment.

* *We learn how to read time, but not how to value it.*

It's tragic when a
person becomes a
worse version of themselves after
they've been loved.

* *You did not have to do much, but*
  you still managed to become ungrateful.

Are we more than
just together?

Do you love being with
me?

Does time feel different without
me?

Do I move your heart?

Do I excite you on a normal day?

Do you want to look at me when
you are?

Do you find it strange when we
don't hold hands?

Do you like listening to me, so
you can try to understand?

Do I make a difference?

Do you love me?

* *You are not the monster I always feared, but*
  I am learning to fear that
  you do not love me.

Don't open me in places you want nothing to do with
afterwards.

If you did not intend flowers, you
should not have nurtured me
like the sun and moon.

If you did not intend magic, you
should not have touched me.
Am I the only one responsible for my body
when you also said you loved me?

If you did not want 'forever', you
should not have spoken like it, even
if you didn't say the word.

If this was not love, why
did you behave like it was?

If moving on was easy for you, why
did you make it hard for me?

I am talking about everything you
said.
Everything you did.
The happiness that was more visible than
my face.
The dreams we spoke about.
You, who were never mine.

— Answer

In the end, I was left begging for mercy.

You spiralled out of control and
I chased you with unanswered questions.
But you were already making 'healthier' choices that
conveniently avoided accountability.

You buried me where I spoke and
did not cry over it.

You moved on but kept me suspended in
the anxiety of when you'd end it for me too.
My system, traumatised.

Yet, you found it brutal that everyone asked whether
you still loved me or not.

Even so, I was still there for you.
But you accused my intentions to absolve yourself.

Nobody changes this much.
You only revealed who you are.

In my position, I could
only beg for mercy because
I could not do to you what
you were doing to me, nor
could I let you get away with
what you were doing to me.

* *It takes heart to beg, and it takes a heart to have mercy.*

In your eyes, you're not making her a mother.
In your eyes, you're making her worthless.

But now she's worth more
in body, soul, and status.

She is outgrowing you.

* *You could have shared in the rewards.*

Don't take her voice and mind personal.

Her existence does not make you less of a man.

It makes a whole
generation.

* *Be in her league.*

I caught the illness of aging.

My shoulders dropped from the will to
live this life, nor
ready for the next.
The colours of my face turned pale before
your strange moods.
My dark circles grew, burying
what I witnessed of you.
I lost hair most quietly, somewhere among
shortened days and
long nights.
My hips stiffened when you were around.
My bones complained of you.
Always gasping for air.
I ached everywhere.

I caught the illness of aging.

— Toxic

Love can come with a demand that
you stay at home, while
they're out with
anyone new or old.

They know where you are, but
you never know how close or far
they might be.
They know everything about you, but
you only know as much as they allow you to.

No matter how they choose to love, you
must love better.
No matter how much they trust, you
must trust more.

— Conditions

There were no burnt cigarettes, but he put me at many risks.
There were no bottles, but he treated me badly enough.
There was no violence, but I feared the next words coming
out of his mouth that
would break my core.

What he did was invisible.
There were no signs of
what he was doing.

Yet, I looked defeated.

But my heart was signalling otherwise;
it had never given up to
the years, the damage, or on me.

Time passed, courage steadied and faltered many times before I
finally took a leap of faith having come a lifetime of a way.

* *It's never too late to want better.*

I give you the silent treatment because
you treat me with worse.

But you still continue to attack me.

You set off a chain of events and
pretend like you don't know what's happening, trying
to gaslight your way out of it all, making
me feel insane for knowing the truth.

You can't make me look past what you've realised but
don't want to admit.

* *I can see through you.*

You tell the woman you just hurt how much she means to you.

You sweet-talk the woman you just put through hell.

You take to dinner the woman you just broke.

You make promises to the woman you just cheated on.

You give flowers to the woman you just beat up.

You make love to the woman you just hated on.

You are sorry to the woman who trusted you.

You cry to the woman who is about to leave.

You give explanations to a woman you have confused.

— Crimes

You hurt me, took your time, and
have now come back.

You walk into my peace, claiming
your spot again.

But when I was hurt and you were gone, you
became a blur in my memories.

You faded from the brief time we had, as if
we were never significant at any point in time.

* I took the pain as if it would matter forever.

I am a woman, but
like a kid, I was under your control.

You didn't want to be my man
and lead.
You wanted to be in control
of me.

— Toxic Masculinity

I paid for what you have.

You traded me and everything you made me believe in.

I never knew I was worth so much, yet so cheap.

You were right about some of the misfortunes I would face, because you saw someone close to you go through it.

Yet, you did it to me anyway.

You knew what could become of my fate and every vulnerable outcome you had left me to.

I still asked what if something happens to me? You had the audacity to tell me that "that's life."

And you were so confident that you would be okay.

You consoled me that I'd be okay too if only I go through the pain already.
And I did like a failed
human lab-rat that
you turned into an emotional freak.
I didn't know who I had become.

Every path I took to find myself led me back to Allah, because He is closer to us than we are to ourselves.

* *You dehumanised me to*
  make your dreams come true.

  You will never be the same again.

I reject everything you did for me the way you rejected me at
my lowest.

You did not feel the same as
before I was tainted by a mistake that wasn't only mine.

Yet, I bore the consequences with
every ounce of my dignity.
But you still found it unruly that I was reacting.

I lost layers of myself within weeks.
You advised me to get professional help when
I came to you.

It was no longer a matter of us but rather
what was practical for you.
I poured my heart out against
your logic that assessed the potential losses and gains of
giving us another chance.
I was broken, but you were fixated on
worldly affairs.
I had become a liability.

You finally apologised without
admitting to much and
let me go in
your own time.

I'll remember that you were the one who knew everything
about me, and yet you did what you did with no mercy.

I reject everything you did for me the way you rejected me at
my lowest.

* *Some of the most painful rejections become the best redirections.*

You brought the child out in me, and
I loved you with innocence, excitement, and blind belief.

I spoke to you more openly than I did to my mother—reassured.
I felt with you how I never felt with my father—anchored.

You loved me with priority.

But you left, and
I realised days later.

You explained what you wanted,
ignored what made you uneasy,
shut down any accountability,
and cut me off at guilt, as
you grasped at straws.

I lost my mind somewhere between
life and fiction.

But you remained brutally civil in response—careful about
giving me hope for you had your own plans.

The pain became paralysing.
But your silence was set in stone.

* *You uprooted me from the spine.
But a friend of mine told me that
one of the realest human experiences is to
feel.*

Don't judge me for my silence.

You have no idea how much my heart has stretched to make space for every type of pain that became transformative.

You don't know how dangerously low my mind has travelled to realise that Allah is greater than where I ended up.

You don't know how many times I took my first breath surviving one breakdown, after another.

You don't know of all the things I have thought of and sat with to slowly and painstakingly find the words to turn them into a comprehendible sentence and find some relief in finally making sense of them.

You don't know, that for a while, I lived life seeing through the illusion of everything, trying to find it tasteful again.

You don't know how grateful I have become for every small joy because everything is so fragile.

You don't know that I had to make it possible to move on without an apology from anyone.

You don't understand that I cannot hurt you, because you decided that hurting me was the only way out for you.

Don't judge me for my silence.

You don't deserve to know what happened to me, what I know today, and the tale I have become.

* *Some stories spread in silence because their victory make all the noise.*

You took your love away from me, but
it did not make me ugly.

I still told you to live,
to take care of yourself,
and to try again.

* *I did not take you down with me.*

This is how I will rise again.

Growth

I don't want to figure out the complexities of my mum,
destroying myself.

Her past taunts me, haunting me in my
sleep paralysis. I sweat more than I breathe, trying to
speak, scream, move, and break free from
a reality I block out to evade the ultimate guilt of
what I did not commit, yet I must make up for, and surpass.

All eyes are on me with every step I take, doubting the past
figures I
may replicate.
But I don't believe in the rumours.

I will be better.
I will be better without competing with your past or
who you have become, mama.
I will be better without taking undue accountability that others
have put on me.
I will be better without sacrificing my dreams.
I will be better for us, and
in the end, you will be the happiest for me.

* Breaking trauma, not another generation.

Mental Health is beautiful to have and painful to lose.

* *What may not be your fault can still be in your hands.*

Don't give up on yourself.

"I'm going to hurt myself.", they say.

And suddenly, I feel like I'm in the
hospital emergency room within
my own house, and
the person I love is fighting between
life and death.
I tell them to choose life.
I make them choose life.
I fight for their life.

— The Stories of Carers

You want to bridge our age gap
at any cost.

And while you're trying to match me with no remorse, you're
creating more distance than
the one I do not care for.

You look past me and raise your voice when
you don't need me, so you can feel
independent again.

You go after everything I do for you, thinking
you know what you're accusing me of.

I want you to know that
I did not choose to be born like this—older than you, a privilege
that would make me fold myself over the years, so I don't offend
someone in my own
house.

Yet, you treat me as an obstacle in your
space.

There is one thing I did choose:
that you have it better than I did.
But you taunt me that I'm not the only one who
has endured.
Though, I do not live with this narrative.

And no matter how old we become, I will always be
older than you, and
there for you
for as long as I live.

* *Sibling rivalry is fun young.*

If you want to judge me, I have judged myself a
thousand times.

I have looked in a mirror more
daring than the sun.

So, the changes came heavily.

I didn't want to leave, but
I was holding on to something I had lost and
was still losing myself to.

So, if you want to judge me, I have judged myself a
thousand times.

I have looked in a mirror more
daring than the sun.

It was hard to wake up to normal days again—not paralysed by
pain, nor possessed with
vengeance, but sitting still,
figuring out forgiveness for both sides;
holding on tight for survival, yet letting go of myself;
in denial, yet learning from it all.

So, if you want to judge me, I have judged myself a
thousand times.

I have looked in a mirror more
daring than the sun.

* *I've seen the colours in me.*

You matter in this life.
You're here to experience.

Your life matters.
There's still some time and forgiveness left.

You matter.
Come out of your hiding to
your purpose.

Your story makes a difference to
those who will be in your position one day.

Feel the hurt without
punishing yourself.
It needs a way out, not back in.

Ride the waves.
Be beautiful in everything you do.
Give it time.
Have faith.
Things will work out.

* *You have a role to play in the moments before the turning point.*

I am quiet, but in my mind it's loud.

The noise is stuck and continuous.

It keeps me up and I wake up with it.

I work different parts of me harder than
my thoughts.

I want out.

My will is clear and strong.

* *The mind is not made to control more than it is made to let go,
and this is one of the most powerful acts of self-control.*

Actions speak louder than words, but
intentions speak louder than actions.

Don't give and
boast.
Don't help and
remind.
Don't love and
disrespect.

Doing good doesn't give you authority over people's
vulnerabilities.

Be there for others with humility, for they elevate you in more
ways than you alleviate their troubles.

Treat people better after
you love them.

Actions speak louder than words, but
intentions speak louder than actions.

— Make it Count

It's in times of darkness and utmost vulnerability that sometimes, the closest people will start living their 'own lives'.

It's heart-breaking. It's discouraging. It's scary and difficult to comprehend the resignation of those closest to you in your time of need.
It's hard being the one adapting to the convenience of others when your life has taken a blow and a turn.
You're holding it down for everyone when you can barely hold yourself together.

Know that this is strength.
Know that not only can you withstand such an off-putting and gruelling human experience, but you can outgrow your situation, forgive them, and one day, turn up better, even for those who didn't turn up for you.

You must own who you are regardless of others.

— An Open Heart

Kind people are not blind people.

They know the world like
you do.
But they don't confront you like
others.

They are people who make excuses for you.

Sometimes, they pretend like it doesn't hurt.

They don't leave soon enough.

But they can change if you don't.

They can see you for who you are.

They can judge.

They can attack back.

They can choose to leave.

Kind people are not blind people.

They know the world like
you do.

— Kind, Not Blind

To be needed but not loved is
depriving.

Accepting parts of me but not all has
conditioned me for whoever walks into
my life.

I am sharing myself with those who
do not deserve me.

I am fighting to keep people.

— The Battle of Self Worth

I wanted to be discovered and
valued.
So, I supplied.

But people still didn't see me.

It was not them.
It was me.

While I believed in being merciful towards
The Almighty's creation, I didn't realise that
I am also a part of His creation.

I am responsible for myself too.

* *You don't need to drop others to love yourself, and you don't
  need to forget yourself to love others.*

The Bigger Picture

They broke you and
replaced your broken pieces with
someone else.

This is probably one of the most grievous of human experiences.

You've been cut open without
anaesthesia.
Your eyes are as open as
your wound.

Feeling has become traumatic.

You're breaking in places you
never even knew could bend.
But here you are, opening up instead of
denying yourself the pain.

What an end to your trust, but
not your life.

Do not think yourself finished.
New beginnings often feel like
the end of everything.

You are not a reflection of what
happened to you.
So, stop pretending flaws.

It's about life. Life has its ups and downs.
It has its trials and ease.
What happens to you does not stick with you.
What you do with it will.

Life will take you far away from the incident.
It will move on, take you to different places, show you what's

out there, teach you new experiences, and maybe
reveal to you why things happened the
way they did.

But you need to take the baby steps in the
right direction.

Do not wait.

Go after what you can still save, have, and become.

— The Bigger Picture

I'd keep people as a trauma response.

I sought warmth from different characters.
I sought validation from those who
couldn't even apologise.

I'd go back and
try to do more because
I was broken enough.

I did not know a love, a bond, and security beyond
this.

I attached myself to whoever let me stay.

* *I did the scariest thing and let go, grounding myself with
hope.*

I said nothing to
see what people would do.

No one sat with me.

No one asked me anything.

No one cancelled their plans.

No one cut me any slack
even on the weekends.

No one broke the ice on
a special occasion.

No one new came for me.

When I did say something
no one took accountability.

* *Sometimes, you are compelled to face a situation alone, because
  your victory will come from Allah alone.*

I suffered.
I listened.
I forgave.
I stayed.

I was still told to let them know if
I ever might need them.

You can't force people to stay in your life, nor can you force
yourself to hate anyone.

* *What may seem like a rejection, may be someone fighting their
demons away from you. It's less about you, and more about what
they need to do for themselves. Wish them well.*

A broken vision cannot be reduced to a
broken heart.

A broken vision is
everything bad you've ever seen, heard of, and
thought could not happen to you, happen
to you.

A broken vision no longer judges the bad ones because the good
ones do bad things too.

A broken vision is
knowing that not all justice is served in
this world.

A broken vision is content because
the peace within is greater than the
chaos outside.

A broken vision does not ache or long like a
broken heart, because the illusion leaves with
all the losses.

A broken vision lives with the hereafter in
sight.

A broken vision sees beyond the broken things.

True change comes from within, not
for someone else.

Changing for someone else comes with
unwanted noise.
It's a little misguided,
half-hearted,
half-learnt, and
short-lived.

Changing from within is
true.
It comes from a long-lost, innate understanding.
It's relatable.
It's freeing.

— Change

When you have God's promise, you
don't need anyone's
reciprocation or commitment, because
the most promising distinction between
God and people is that He
responds.

* *You're covered.*

— Security

No knife can cut through how
you feel.
No noose is long enough to
tell your story.
No rooftop is high enough to
take your falls.
No drink comforts as much as it abuses.
No overdose can
fight your problems.
No deep water can
drown you and save you at
the same time.
There's nothing like
the morning brightness.
I understand that the nights are hard to get through, not so much
because of the lack of light, but because they are idle.
What can you solve in stillness?
You can only put it to rest when
you can't see, understand, or do a thing.
And you are
loved mightily.
You made it here because
every trial had an end.
So, trust the process.
After every hardship, what is to come is
better.
Patience is bitter, but it will leave you in awe of a
beautiful end.
To hope is to believe in good things for yourself.
Breathe in, breathe out, breathe on.

— Stay

Heal.
Don't tread wrong paths.
Heal.
Don't envy.
Heal.
Don't hurt others.
Heal.
Don't destroy yourself.
Heal.
Don't lose hope.
Heal.

* *Don't kill yourself over what
   only hurt you.*

It's normal to overcome adversity.

Have you seen the person who always laughs and smiles but whose past shocks us?

Have you befriended the one who will believe you despite having been betrayed by every person who was supposed to protect them.

Do you know the one who cheers for everyone, yet no one celebrated their wins.

Have you met the person who lost everyone they loved, and yet they never stopped giving.

Have you been around the one whose life has been a severe trial, but their heart is tranquil and firm in faith.

There are beautiful people who have carried their loved one's dead bodies and pieces.

Those who are waiting for justice without wronging others.

Those whose foresight we cannot comprehend.

There are humans who are dehumanised.

Yet, none of them behave entitled.

Trials are meant to humble you.

To know hardship is to know humility.

To have learnt the hard way is to empathise with others.

To have made it to the other side is to be grateful.

— Modesty

Make peace with being tested in this world
because Allah has a right to test us.

This will keep you grounded in many situations
because you know the purpose of life
is to worship Him.

And if you're able to strive for the hereafter, doors will open for
you here too.

The Prophet (peace and blessings of Allah be upon him) said
that if the final hour is about to be established and you have a
shoot of a plant in your hands, then still plant it if it's possible.

You should try to finish every good you start.

Not even the coming of the final hour should stop you.

— The Dreams and Tests of This World

I have wishes I am
praying and working
for.

So, please do not approach me to lead me astray and
away from my
dreams.

— Sins Become Barriers

Speaking up can be patience.
Silence can be oppressive.

Not all that makes noise is
crazy.
Not all that is silent should be
praised.

* *Justice has many volumes.*

Faith and hope come together.

To be without hope is
to be without faith.

Faith allows us to believe in anything, while
hope allows us to keep believing.

We have one to hold onto when
the other becomes weak.

They are put together to
keep us from giving up as
believers.

* *Your support system.*

I will not become the witch, the
addict, bitter, or
loose.

I will keep my heart beautiful even
if my life looks otherwise.

And I don't need anyone to understand me.

I don't need to connect with anybody on
my art.

* *I will believe in my own work.*

Like a revert to Islam or a convert, if you like, a born Muslim can also have a change of heart.

Although you've had your own way for years, an epiphany can happen to you too.
Your heart can be turned.
Your senses can be elevated.

You may understand a message that you've come across many times, but this feels like the first time.

You realise that it was never a choice between life or Islam, because Islam is a way of life;
not for you to be perfect, but
to sincerely try.

Like a revert to Islam or a convert, if you like, a born Muslim can also have a change of heart.

— A Born Muslim

There are many sources of darkness, but
there is only one source of light.

This may seem scarce, but it is
abundant.

Because it is from
Allah.

Allah is the light of the heavens, the earth, and
whatever is in between.

Imagine being deprived of a light this generous?

— Light of All Worlds

The pain my heart carries is for nothing but to
get closer to You.
The prison within me is for nothing but to
break free to You.
This restlessness is for nothing but to
find peace with You.
I'm holding myself together in front of the
whole world but
letting go to You, where I hold
value.

* *I am nothing even in my worship of You.*
But I hope that You accept even as much as
nothing from me out of Your mercy on me.

Whatever may overcome me does not really matter.
Whoever may overwhelm me, it's not personal.
In truth, they are just excuses.
They are mere illusions for what really matters—everything
between me and You.

Will I still remember You or not?
Will I still have hope?
Will I still believe?
Will I still think good of You.
Will I be patient?
How beautiful will my patience be?

All else
is easy
for You.

If You want, You can change a heart, and
if You want, You can change a situation.
It is all easy for You.
You are near and
so is Your help.

* *Everything is divine matter.*

People judge that the miserable who
have nothing going for them usually choose God and His path.

But how many times have we chosen people and told them
about our past only to be put through the same thing or
worse?

* *Judge me again.*

Only Allah knows about the slightest glance, what is in a heart, and what the soul whispers.

No one can perceive you, come through, and heal you as best as He is able to.

Validating something that's even the weight of a mustard seed is important to Him, let alone tears, heartbreak, trauma, sleepless nights, overdue apologies, and lost time.

Everything will be accounted for.

— The Weight of a Mustard Seed

One day, your mental health will be more on your side.

Things will not be perfect, but
they will be better.

You will have space to feel.

You will no longer be afraid to
decide something.

You will live with dignity.

You will have a story to tell.

Have firm faith in Allah, keep trying, and
take breaks.

* *It's not over yet.*

Don't lose focus.

Allah does not need you.
You need Him.

If you decide to forget Him, He will replace you, and
this will be your biggest regret, because there's no greater calling
than His.

So, ask Him to use you for His cause.

Ask Him to use you for something greater than
what you're grieving.

Watch Him give you the upper hand.

You are not a lost cause.

Allah is precise in all matters.
Nothing is an accident.

Inspiration

Stay

Stay takes inspiration from surah 93 of the Qur'an, Ad-Duhaa, which is translated as "The Morning Sunlight" by Dr. Mustafa Khattab, whose translation of the Qur'an I will cite from quran.com.

Before this surah was revealed, some scholars say that prophet Muhammad (peace and blessings of Allah be upon him) received no revelation from Allah for around six months, while others say that weeks or days had passed. Nevertheless, this gap in receiving no revelation led prophet Muhammad (peace and blessings of Allah be upon him) to doubt himself, wondering what he may have done wrong to displease Allah (Alkauthar Institute, 2012). He began to believe that he was no longer worthy of Allah's love, and that Allah did not want him (as a prophet) anymore. Understandably, these thoughts caused him great grief.

Thus, surah Ad-Duhaa was revealed to relieve prophet Muhammad (peace and blessings of Allah be upon him) from his insecurities. The surah starts with Allah saying, "By the morning sunlight" (verse 93:1), which immediately brightens up the situation, shifting the perspective from negative to positive, while emphasising on a new day, akin to a new beginning. Usually, when someone is low in mood, depressed, or experiencing trauma, their ability to recognise the positive aspects in their situation or environment depreciates. Therefore, it's useful to remind people of the brighter things in life, prompting one to take a step back from their own perception and start afresh, as symbolised by sunlight and incorporated in *Stay*, "There's nothing like the morning brightness."

Allah then says, "And the night when it falls still!" (verse 93:2). The night is supposed to be the calm (or "still") hours of the day. However, when in distress, we often use this time to ruminate and magnify our problems. *Stay* highlights this notion, validating the distress people face particularly at night. However, night itself is for rest and to soothe anxieties, and so, Allah mentions the still night as a means for us to seek comfort in, which *Stay* encourages, "I understand that the nights are hard to get through, not so much because of the lack of light, but because they are idle. What can you solve in stillness? You can only put it to rest when you can't see, understand, or do a thing."

The surah goes on to address the feeling of being 'hated' in verse 93:3, "Your Lord [O prophet] has not abandoned you, nor has He become hateful [of you]." Feeling hated is, for obvious reasons, very unpleasant, especially by someone we seek love and approval from. It can feel devaluing and lead us to develop self-doubt in our being and in our efforts. So, with Allah proclaiming that He is not displeased with prophet Muhammad (peace and blessings of Allah be upon him), He is sending a message of His approval and love, thus removing his self-doubt and restoring his self-value. *Stay* states, "You are loved mightily," inspired by this verse to remind us of our value, remove self-doubt, and to keep us firm in our good endeavours.

Lastly, surah Ad-Duhaa provides comfort as Allah tells prophet Muhammad (peace and blessings of Allah be upon him), "And [surely] your Lord will give so much to you that you will be pleased." (verse 93:5). To reaffirm His promise, Allah reminds prophet Muhammad (peace and blessings of Allah be upon him) of examples from his earlier life in verses 93:6-93:8, noting how He changed his hardships into favourable situations. *Stay* provides this assurance that "after every hardship, what is to come is better."

Stay is also partly inspired by surah 12, named after prophet Yusuf, *Joseph*, (peace be upon him). Verse 12:87 states, "O my sons! Go and search diligently for Joseph and his brother. And do not lose hope in the mercy of Allah, for no one loses hope in Allah's mercy except those with no faith." Here, Yaqub, *Jacob*, (peace be upon him), who is also a prophet, addresses his sons who once threw their brother, prophet Yusuf (peace be upon him), to the bottom of a well and abandoned him when he was a little boy. This verse instructs them to rectify their mistake years later when Yusuf (peace be upon him) would be a grown man, and while doing so, to put their hope in the mercy of Allah. This message is incredibly humbling and a morale boost as it tells us not to despair and fall victim to our own sins and mistakes, but rather to make things right and to put our hope in Allah for relief, as *Stay* encourages, "To hope is to believe in good things for your-self."

Finally, *Stay* touches on having patience, "Patience is bitter, but it will leave you in awe of a beautiful end". In the Qur'an, Allah repeatedly encourages people to be patient when facing hardship. This, however, does not go unreciprocated or unrewarded, as He says in surah Al-Baqara, "O believers! Seek comfort in patience and prayer. Allah is truly with those who are patient." (verse 2:153).

The Dreams and Tests of This World

In the Musnad Ahmad collection of hadith, Anas Ibn Malik reports that prophet Muhammad (peace and blessings of Allah be upon him) said, "If the final hour comes while you have a shoot of a plant in your hands and it is possible to plant it before the hour comes, you should plant it." (in Attending to this world, n.d). This is because Islam rewards planting as an act of charity, as it provides food and/or shade to animals and humans. Importantly, any good deed may be rewarded in the hereafter, which is the ultimate goal for a Muslim. Furthermore, this hadith serves as motivation to complete a good task we take on. *The Dreams and Tests of This World* takes inspiration from this to encourage the completion of good work for worldly benefits and success in the hereafter.

* *Your support system.*

This poem is inspired by the aforementioned surah of Yusuf, verse 12:87, which explains that only those with no faith have no hope in Allah's mercy.

The Weight of a Mustard Seed

The opening sentence of this poem, "Only Allah knows about the slightest glance, what is in a heart, and what the soul whispers to you.", is entirely inspired by the Qur'an.

In surah 40, Ghafir, *The Forgiver*, Allah tells us that He has knowledge of even the smallest of our actions which may not be noticeable by others, "Allah even knows the sly glances of the eyes and whatever the hearts conceal." (verse 40:19). Although this verse talks about the fraudulent eyes, the poem takes away the message of Allah's omniscience.

Moving on to "...what is in a heart...", the Qur'an mentions the human heart well over one-hundred times. This includes the inner heart, and the metaphoric term, 'chest', none of which I will directly reference due to the extensive breadth, but please find a list of verses on QP (n.d.).

Some of the verses reveal that the heart is an intelligent organ. It is the root of where intentions are formed, where reasoning takes place, and decisions are made.

In addition to being sentient, Allah reveals that the heart has a health status: either soft (healthy), hard as stone (unhealthy/diseased), or even harder than stone (QP, n.d.). A diseased heart has little to no humane touch, and therefore cannot perceive right and wrong, and is defiant against divine revelation, affecting its reasoning and decision-making. In contrast, a healthy heart is soft, able to perceive right and wrong, is accepting of divine revelation, and therefore makes sound decisions. Allah being our Creator, therefore knows what is in every heart, as *The Weight of a Mustard Seed* acknowledges.

Further to His omniscience, Allah says in surah 50, Qaf, which literally is the letter "qaf" from the Arabic alphabet, "Indeed, it is We Who created humankind and fully know what their souls whisper to them..." (verse 50:16). Meaning, He has complete knowledge of what we think about, whether good, bad, or the struggles we don't speak about out loud. To emphasise that Allah possesses all things in His knowledge, I took inspiration from this verse.

The poem goes on to state, "Validating something that's even the weight of a mustard seed is important to Him." The weight of a mustard seed is used as an example in the Qur'an to show that Allah is firm in upholding justice even to the weight of a mustard seed. In surah 21, Al-Anbya, *The Prophets*, Allah says, "We will set up the scales of justice on the Day of Judgement, so no soul will be wronged in the least. And even if a deed is the weight of a mustard seed, We will bring it forth. And sufficient are We as a vigilant Reckoner." (verse 21:47). This explains that no matter how small a deed may be, it will be brought to account by Allah so that everybody is dealt with absolute justice in every matter, and nobody is wronged in the least. The example of the mustard seed is also given in surah 31, Luqman, named after an individual who some scholars believe to be a prophet, while others believe him to be a righteous man (peace be upon him) gifted with wisdom from Allah. In verse 31:16, Allah says, "Luqman added, 'O my dear son! Even if a deed were the weight of a mustard seed— be it hidden in a rock or in the heavens or the earth—Allah will bring it forth. Surely Allah is Most Subtle, All-Aware.'" This verse makes it clear that nothing is hidden from Allah, no matter how subtle or minute. All deeds will be brought to light.

Sources

AlKauthar Institute. (2012, May 18). *How Surah Ad-Dhuha can change your life - Sh Tawfique Chowdhury [Beautiful]* [Video]. YouTube. https://www.youtube.com/watch?v=KoqhNz7wD3I

Attending to this world - كتاب الاعتناء بالدنيا - Sunnah.com - Sayings and Teachings of Prophet Muhammad (صلى الله عليه و سلم). (n.d.). https://sunnah.com/urn/2304770

Ad-Duhaa – 93:1 - Quran.com. (n.d.). Quran.com. https://quran.com/93/1

Ad-Duhaa – 93:2 - Quran.com. (n.d.). Quran.com. https://quran.com/93/2

Ad-Duhaa – 93:3 - Quran.com. (n.d.). Quran.com. https://quran.com/93/3

Ad-Duhaa – 93:5 - Quran.com. (n.d.). Quran.com. https://quran.com/93/5

Ad-Duhaa – 93:6 - Quran.com. (n.d.). Quran.com. https://quran.com/93/6

Ad-Duhaa – 93:7 - Quran.com. (n.d.). Quran.com. https://quran.com/93/7

Ad-Duhaa – 93:8 - Quran.com. (n.d.). Quran.com. https://quran.com/93/8

Al-Ahzab- 33:56 - Quran.com. (n.d.). Quran.com.
https://quran.com/en/al-ahzab/56

Al-Anbya – 21:47 - Quran.com. (n.d.). Quran.com.
https://quran.com/21/47

Al-Baqara – 2:153 - Quran.com (n.d.). Quran.com.
https://quran.com/2/153

Al-Baqara – 2:263 - Quran.com (n.d.). Quran.com.

https://quran.com/2/263

Ghafir – 40:19 - Quran.com. (n.d.-b). Quran.com.
https://quran.com/ghafir/19

Ibrahim – 14:24 - Quran.com. (n.d.-b). Quran.com.

https://quran.com/14/24

Ibrahim – 14:25 - Quran.com. (n.d.-b). Quran.com.

https://quran.com/14/25

Ibrahim – 14:26 - Quran.com. (n.d.-b). Quran.com.

https://quran.com/14/26

Ibrahim – 14:27 - Quran.com. (n.d.-b). Quran.com.

https://quran.com/14/27

Luqman – 31:16 - Quran.com. (n.d.). Quran.com.
https://quran.com/31/16

Qaf – 50:16 - Quran.com. (n.d.). Quran.com.
https://quran.com/en/qaf/16

QP. (n.d.-b). https://www.quranproject.org/The-human-heart-in-the-glorious-Quran-481-d

Quran.com. (2024). https://quran.com/

Yusuf – 12:87 - Quran.com. (n.d.). Quran.com. https://quran.com/12/87

Milton Keynes UK
Ingram Content Group UK Ltd.
UKHW022124100924
1572UKWH00082B/564